CONTENTS

D0479611

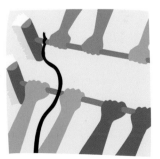

Getting started

Have you ever wondered why things move the way they do? What makes them start moving? Why do things fall when you drop them? Why is swimming so much harder than walking? You will discover the answers to these questions, and many others, in this book. It is packed full of experiments for you to try that will help you understand forces and motion.

Feel the force

Every time you ride a bike, turn a doorknob, or even just move your arm, you are using forces. They are the invisible pushes and pulls that make everything happen.

Athletes, dancers, race car drivers, and engineers all need to understand forces. Every machine, from a seesaw to the space shuttle, relies on forces to work. From the tiny forces that hold atoms together to the huge forces that keep the planets in orbit around the sun, forces really are everywhere!

What you need

You can find most of the things you need for the activities in this book around your house or garage. If you do not have exactly the item shown in the picture, you can probably use something similar that will do the same thing. These activities may give you ideas for other experiments you can try. As long as they are safe (ask an adult), try them out! Improvisation is part of the fun.

Most of the activities use empty containers. Start saving plastic bottles, tubs, and cartons. You never know what will come in handy!

Your experiments are more likely to be successful if you work carefully and clean up as you go.

SACRAMENTO PUBLIC LIBRARY

3 0029 04485 6896

RANCHO CORDOVA LIBRARY
9845 FOLSOM BLVD.
SACRAMENTO, CA 95827

07/01

HANDS-ON
Science

Sci Exp label

Forces and Motion

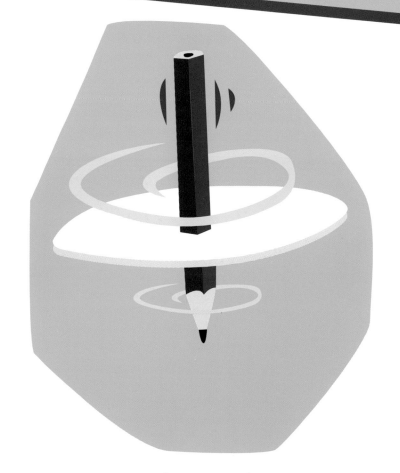

John Graham

Illustrated by David Le Jars

KING*f*ISHER

NEW YORK

RANCHO CORDOVA

KINGFISHER
Larousse Kingfisher Chambers Inc.
95 Madison Avenue
New York, New York 10016
www.kingfisherpub.com

Produced for Kingfisher by PAGE*One*

First published in 2001
10 9 8 7 6 5 4 3 2 1

1TR/1200/TWP/GRST/150SMA

Copyright © Kingfisher Publications Plc 2001

All rights reserved under International and
Pan-American Copyright Conventions

LIBRARY OF CONGRESS CATALOGING-IN-PUBLICATION DATA
has been applied for.

ISBN 0-7534-5348-7

Printed in Singapore

For PAGE*One*
Creative Director Bob Gordon
Project Editor Miriam Richardson
Designers Monica Bratt, Tim Stansfield

For Kingfisher
Managing Editor Clive Wilson
Coordinating Editor Laura Marshall
DTP Coordinator Nicky Studdart

Warning

Read all the steps for an activity before you start. Then follow them carefully—rushing or getting carried away could cause an accident. A pair of scissors or a hammer could cause serious injury. Ask an adult for help. Have fun, but work safely!

Be extra careful when using glue. Make sure you are using the right kind. Follow the instructions and pay attention to any safety warnings. If in doubt, ask an adult.

When working outside, stay away from traffic, open water, overhead power lines, and other hazards. Make sure a responsible adult knows where you are and what you are doing.

Clock symbol

The clock symbol at the beginning of each experiment shows you how many minutes the activity should take. All of the experiments take between 5 and 30 minutes. If you are using glue, allow extra time for drying.

Having problems?

If something doesn't work at first, don't give up.

Look through the instructions and illustrations again to see if there's anything you have missed.

Some of the activities need patience—glue takes time to dry, and sometimes adjustments may be needed to get something to work well.

You don't have to do the experiments in the order they are in the book, although you may find they make a little more sense if you do. You don't have to do every single one, but the more you try, the more you will discover about forces and motion, and the more fun you will have!

Stuck for words?

If you come across a word you don't understand or you just want to find out more, take a look at the glossary on pages 38 and 39.

Measuring forces

Forces are all around us. They are the pushes and pulls that affect the shape of something and how it moves. The strength of a force is measured in newtons (N), named after the English scientist Sir Isaac Newton. On earth, everything has weight. This is the force of gravity pulling things down. Most people weigh things in pounds or kilograms. But because weight is a force, it should really be measured in newtons. On earth, a 3½-ounce (100-g) mass has a weight of 1N. A one-pound (0.5-kg) mass has a weight of 4.5N.

Make a force meter

It is easy to make a force meter that measures the force of gravity.

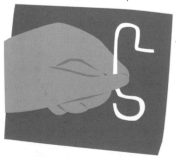

YOU WILL NEED
20
◆ A LARGE YOGURT TUB OR OTHER PLASTIC CONTAINER
◆ STRING
◆ TWO BIG PAPER CLIPS
◆ A LONG, STRONG RUBBER BAND
◆ PAPER, A MARKER, AND A RULER
◆ A FEW FULL PACKAGES OF FOOD WITH THEIR MASS IN OUNCES ON THEIR LABELS
◆ A SKEWER

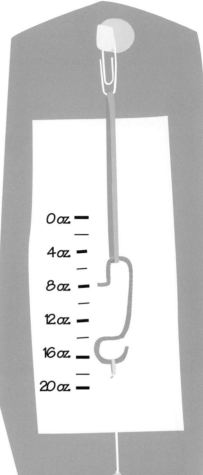

1 Find a hook or something you can hang your force meter from, and attach a piece of paper to the wall below it. Loop the rubber band into a paper clip and hang the clip from the hook.

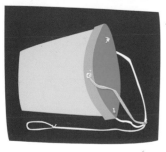

2 Open the other paper clip to make a hook at one end and a pointer at the other. You may need some help and a pair of pliers.

3 Punch holes around the rim of the tub and use string to make a handle. Hang the tub from the rubber band with the bent paper clip.

4 Put the packages of food into the tub one at a time. Mark the position of the pointer each time and write the weight next to it to make a scale. Don't overload the tub, or the rubber band will snap! To turn your scale into newtons, divide each weight in ounces by 3.5. For example, a 7-oz. package has a weight of 2N.

What's happening?
Things have weight because gravity pulls on them. Weight is really the force of gravity on something. The stronger the pull of gravity on an object, the more it weighs. The force meter works because the heavier a thing is, the more it stretches the elastic band.

Newton's apple

Big discoveries are sometimes made by chance. Sir Isaac Newton was a scientist who lived in England 300 years ago. Legend says that he was sitting in his garden when he saw an apple fall from a tree. He realized that there must have been an invisible force pulling the apple down toward the earth. He wondered if this force, called gravity, affected the moon, the stars, and the planets, too. Now we know it does. Newton's ideas about gravity completely changed our understanding of the universe.

ON A DIFFERENT SCALE
To figure out your weight in newtons, multiply your mass in pounds by 4.5. On the moon, you would only weigh one sixth as much. Your mass wouldn't change, but in the moon's weaker gravity, you would weigh less.

Make a weighing scale

Put the spring or sponge into the big cake pan, then place the small pan on top. Put the bag of sugar into the small pan. On the outside of the small pan, mark "5 lbs." level with the edge of the big tin. Use other heavy things to make a scale. To make a newton scale, multiply the weight in pounds by 4.5.

YOU WILL NEED
10
◆ TWO DEEP, EMPTY CAKE PANS, ONE SMALLER THAN THE OTHER
◆ A LARGE SPRING FROM AN OLD MATTRESS OR CHAIR, OR A LARGE SPONGE
◆ A 5-LB. BAG OF SUGAR
◆ A WASHABLE MARKER

SUGAR
5 LB.

What happens to the spring when you put the objects in?

What's happening?

This time, instead of stretching a rubber band, the force of gravity is squashing a spring. The more mass an object has, the more strongly gravity pulls down on it, and the more the spring gets squashed.

Squeezing and twisting

Forces can make things change shape. Whenever something is bent, twisted, squashed, or stretched, a force is acting on it. Springy or elastic materials try to go back to their original shape when the force that made them change shape is taken away. This means they can store up energy and then release it to make things move. Wind-up toys and some watches work like this.

Wind-up toy

This toy shows how the energy stored in a twisted rubber band can cause movement.

YOU WILL NEED
- A SPOOL
- A SMALL RUBBER BAND
- TWO TOOTHPICKS
- TAPE
- A CANDLE
- A KNIFE

20

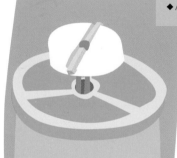

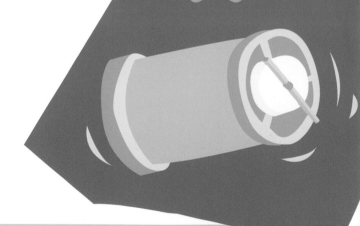

4 Wind up your toy by holding the spool and turning the long toothpick around and around. Put it down and watch it crawl!

1 Cut a thin slice from the wick end of the candle. Make the hole in the middle of the slice (where the wick was) big enough for the rubber band to fit through. Cut a groove in one side.

2 Poke the rubber band through the hole. Put a toothpick through the loop and pull on the other end of the rubber band so the toothpick fits into the groove. One end should reach just past the edge of the spool. Thread the long end of the rubber band through the spool.

3 Push half a toothpick through the rubber band loop at the other end of the spool. Tape the toothpick to the spool to keep it from turning.

What's happening?

As you use a turning force to twist the rubber band, you are storing up energy. Scientists call this potential energy. When you let go, the rubber band unwinds. This turns the toothpick leg and pushes the toy along. The potential energy in the twisted rubber band is turned back into movement energy.

 Spring launcher

Attach the stick to the edge of a table with a blob of modeling clay. Slide the spiral onto the stick, then add the spool. Press the spool down on the spiral and let go. How far can you make it fly? What happens if you give the spool more mass by sticking modeling clay onto it?

What's happening?
The squashed spring stores energy. When released, it uses the energy to push the spool. When mass is added to the spool, you need more force to make it go the same distance.

Roll back
Carefully make two holes in the lid and two holes in the bottom of the box. Cut the rubber band, then thread it through the holes and tie as shown. Tie the weight where the rubber band crosses over and press the lid on. Now gently roll the box forward and let go.

YOU WILL NEED 10
◆ A LARGE, CYLINDRICAL OATMEAL CONTAINER
◆ A LONG RUBBER BAND
◆ A HEAVY NUT OR SIMILAR WEIGHT
◆ STRING
◆ SCISSORS

What happens when you let go?

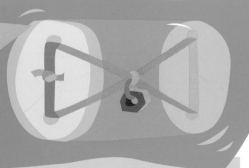

What's happening?
As the cylinder rolls, the nut stays hanging below the rubber band, making it twist. The energy stored in the twisted rubber band drives the cylinder toward you when you let go.

PORTABLE POWER
This portable radio never needs batteries! Instead, it has a crank that is turned by hand to store energy in a big spring. As the spring slowly unwinds, it turns a little generator that powers the radio for about 20 minutes at a time. The radio is especially useful in remote places.

Gravity

Everything is attracted to everything else by the force of gravity, but the attraction between everyday things is too weak to notice. We only feel gravity pulling things down toward the ground so strongly because the earth has a lot of mass. The more mass something has, the stronger its gravitational pull. The moon has less mass than the earth, so gravity is weaker there. Nobody is sure what causes gravity, but without it we would all go flying off into space!

Antigravity cones

You would normally expect things to roll downhill. Or would you?

YOU WILL NEED
10
◆ THICK CARDBOARD
◆ TWO SEMICIRCLES OF THIN CARDBOARD
◆ A RULER AND A PENCIL
◆ TAPE
◆ SCISSORS

Are the cones really defying gravity?

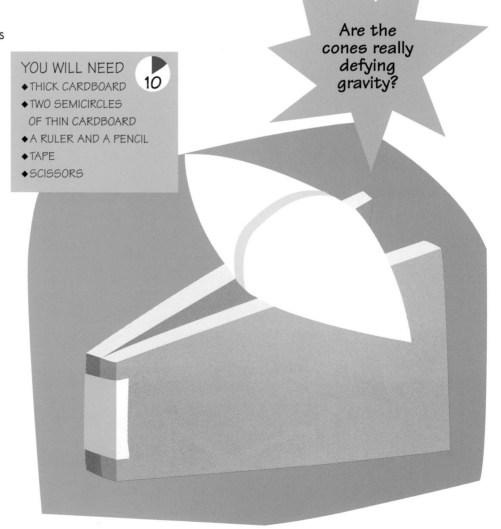

1 Cut two pieces of thick cardboard into the shape shown. Tape the short sides together and open the pieces out slightly, as shown.

2 Roll and tape the semicircles to make two matching cones. Tape the open ends together, as in the picture.

3 Put the cones at the bottom of the hill and watch them appear to defy gravity by rolling uphill!

What's happening?
The cones are not really defying gravity. They are actually going downhill. Watch the middle part carefully. Try measuring the distance from the middle of the cones to the ground at each end of the hill.

Do heavy things fall faster than light ones?

YOU WILL NEED
♦ PAIRS OF THINGS THAT ARE THE SAME
   SIZE AND SHAPE, BUT DIFFERENT WEIGHTS, LIKE:
   A MARBLE AND A BALL BEARING
   A DIE AND A SUGAR CUBE
   A GOLF BALL AND A PING-PONG BALL
♦ TWO CAKE PANS

10

Find something safe to stand on (a sturdy chair will do). Put the pans on the floor, one on either side of you. Then drop both things from each pair from the same height at exactly the same time. Listen for them hitting the pans. Which one lands first? Try repeating your experiment to see if you get the same result every time.

Which object hits the pan first?

What's happening?
Both objects in each pair should land together. Gravity pulls them toward the earth at the same speed, even though they weigh different amounts.

Galileo's story
In the 1590s, an Italian scientist named Galileo Galilei got the idea that things would fall at the same speed no matter how heavy they were. He tested his idea by dropping cannon balls of different weights from the Leaning Tower of Pisa. They always took the same time to hit the ground. Galileo did a lot of scientific experiments. But some of his ideas clashed with what the Catholic Church believed at the time, which got him into trouble!

MOON LIGHT
This picture, taken from a television transmission, shows astronaut David Scott on the moon in 1971. He took the opportunity to test Galileo's theory, this time with a feather and a hammer. There is no air on the moon to slow down the feather, so they both hit the ground at the same time.

Balancing

Something does not have to be moving to have a force acting on it. Gravity is pulling on you now, even if you are sitting still. When all the forces acting on an object cancel each other out, the object is in balance. Every object has a center of gravity. This is the balancing point where the whole weight of the object seems to act. Things with a low center of gravity are very stable. Things with a high center of gravity tend to fall over.

The perching parrot
This parrot will stay on its perch, even when you try to tip it over!

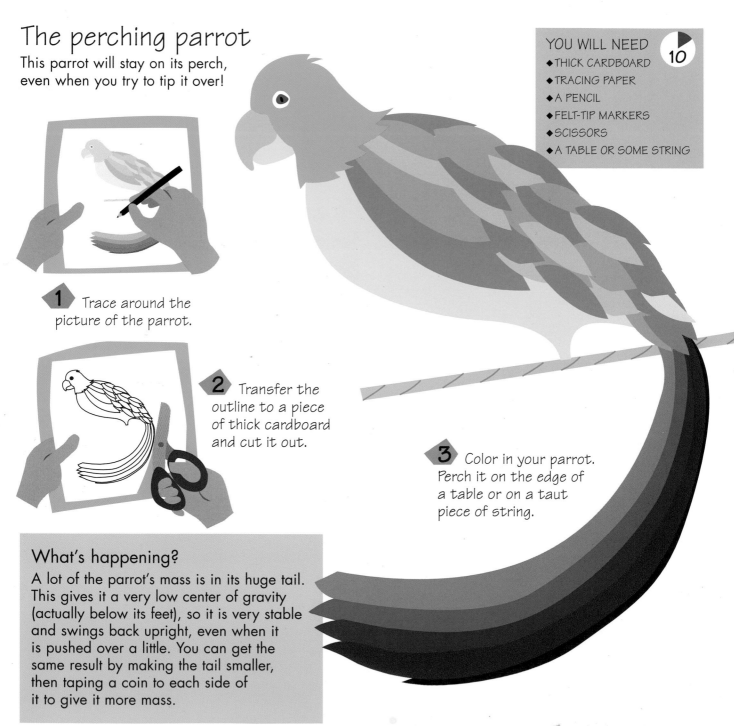

YOU WILL NEED

10

◆ THICK CARDBOARD
◆ TRACING PAPER
◆ A PENCIL
◆ FELT-TIP MARKERS
◆ SCISSORS
◆ A TABLE OR SOME STRING

1 Trace around the picture of the parrot.

2 Transfer the outline to a piece of thick cardboard and cut it out.

3 Color in your parrot. Perch it on the edge of a table or on a taut piece of string.

What's happening?
A lot of the parrot's mass is in its huge tail. This gives it a very low center of gravity (actually below its feet), so it is very stable and swings back upright, even when it is pushed over a little. You can get the same result by making the tail smaller, then taping a coin to each side of it to give it more mass.

Balancing potato

Try to balance a potato on the tip of your finger. Tricky! Now push two metal forks into the potato at an angle, one on each side. Can you balance the potato on your finger now?

YOU WILL NEED
◆ A POTATO
◆ TWO METAL AND TWO PLASTIC FORKS

5

What happens if you use plastic forks?

What's happening?
The mass of the forks moves the potato's center of gravity lower, so it is easier to balance. This does not happen when you use light plastic forks, because they do not have enough mass.

Magic box

Tape the weight into a corner of the box and put the lid on. Slide the box over the edge of a table until only the corner with the weight in it is on the table. The rest of the box seems to be held up by thin air! If you make a false bottom to hide the weight, you can even take the lid off to show that the box is "empty"!

YOU WILL NEED
◆ A SMALL BOX
◆ A HEAVY WEIGHT, OR SEVERAL COINS STUCK TOGETHER
◆ TAPE

5

What's happening?
A box is a regular shape, so you would expect its center of gravity to be in the middle. Adding the weight moves the center of gravity toward the corner. As long as the box's center of gravity is over the table, the box will not fall off. By the way, this also explains why the Leaning Tower of Pisa (page 11) does not fall over.

BALANCING ACT
This tightrope walker is holding a long, flexible pole to lower his center of gravity and make him more stable on the narrow rope. Even so, this act still needs plenty of practice!

Pressure

You can't push your thumb into a cork. But you can easily push a thumbtack into a cork using the same force. This is because the point of the thumbtack concentrates the force onto a tiny area, causing a lot of pressure. The pressure on your thumb is much lower, because the same force is spread out over the tack's big, flat head. The more a force is spread out, the lower the pressure.

Air pressure

The force of the air pressing on things is called air pressure. Although you can't see air pressure, you can see its effect with this quick experiment.

YOU WILL NEED
- A PLASTIC CUP
- A SINK
- AN UNWANTED POSTCARD OR A SHEET OF THIN, STIFF PLASTIC

5

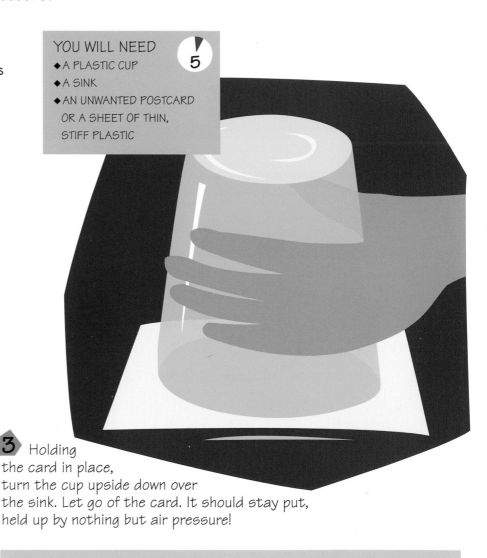

1 Fill the cup right up to the brim with water and slide the card over the top.

3 Holding the card in place, turn the cup upside down over the sink. Let go of the card. It should stay put, held up by nothing but air pressure!

2 Hold the card against the cup with one hand. Hold on to the cup with your other hand.

What's happening?

Air pressure pushes in all directions, including up. It is easily strong enough to hold up the weight of the water in a cup. The card acts as a seal, keeping air out of the cup as you turn it upside down. (Any air left in the cup spoils the trick, because it lets the water pour out.) Air pushes on you, too. In fact, it presses on every square inch of your body with a force of about 15 lb., or 67.5N. You are not crushed because your body pushes back with equal force.

Bed of nails

In 1969, a Hindu fakir named Silki stayed on a bed of nails for 111 days. The secret of his feat has to do with pressure. Although each single nail has a sharp point, there are hundreds of them. The total area of all those points together is enough to reduce the pressure caused by the person's weight so that the nails do not do any harm. The only tricky part is getting on and off!

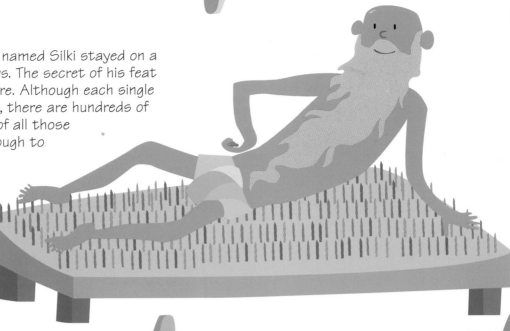

Spread the force

Try pressing a coin into a lump of modeling clay with the flat side down. Then try pressing it in with the edge down. Which is easier?

YOU WILL NEED
- A COIN
- MODELING CLAY

5

What's happening?

The coin is much easier to push in on its edge. The smaller the area, the bigger the pressure caused by the force of your hand. The face of the coin has a much bigger area than the edge, so it spreads the force out and causes a lower pressure.

SPREAD IT AROUND

This tractor's huge tires don't just help it over rough terrain. By spreading the tractor's weight over a large area, they reduce the pressure so the tractor does not sink into the soft ground.

Floating and sinking

Whether something floats or sinks depends on its density. Density measures how heavy something is for its size. For example, a steel cube is a lot heavier than a wooden cube of the same size, so we say that steel is denser than wood. The steel cube sinks in water, but the wooden cube floats. This is because wood is less dense than water—a cube of wood weighs less than a cube of water the same size. So far so good, but then how can a steel ship stay afloat?

Deep-sea diver

You can see how changing an object's density makes it float or sink by making this model of a diver.

YOU WILL NEED
20
◆ A TWO-LITER PLASTIC BOTTLE (WITH CAP)
◆ A FLEXIBLE STRAW
◆ A PAPER CLIP
◆ AN ALUMINUM PIE PLATE
◆ MODELING CLAY
◆ SCISSORS
◆ A BOWL OF WATER

1 Cut out the shape of a diver from the pie plate. Make it tall and thin, about 2 ½ in. (7cm) by ¾ in. (2cm), so it will fit through the neck of the bottle.

2 Bend the straw at the neck, then cut it so you have a U-shaped piece about 1 in. (2.5cm) long. Slide the open ends of the straw onto the two ends of the paper clip.

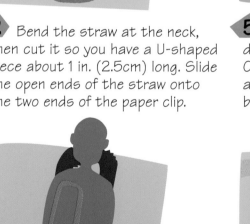

3 Gently slide the paper clip and straw between the diver's legs and up onto its body. The straw should be on its back, bent at the top behind its head, so it looks like a real diver's air tank.

4 Make diving boots out of modeling clay for the diver's feet.

5 Try floating the diver in a bowl of water. Carefully adjust the amount of clay on its boots until it just floats.

6 Fill the bottle with water and put the diver inside. Make sure the bottle is full to the top, then screw the cap on tight. The diver should float to the top.

Can you make your diver float at different depths?

How does a boat float?

Test your objects to see which ones float and which sink. Drop a ball of modeling clay into the water. What happens? Then flatten it out into a bowl shape. Will it float now? Try the same with aluminum foil.

YOU WILL NEED 10

◆ SOME SOLID OBJECTS MADE FROM DIFFERENT MATERIALS, LIKE GLASS, METAL, WOOD, AND PLASTIC
◆ MODELING CLAY
◆ ALUMINUM FOIL
◆ A LARGE BOWL OF WATER

How do the bowl shapes stay afloat?

What's happening?

Small, heavy things, like coins and stones, sink. Large, light things, like corks, float. But when you make a big, hollow boat shape out of something small and heavy, like modeling clay, most of it is actually filled with air. Together, the boat shape and the air inside it are less dense than water, so it floats. This is how steel ships float.

7 Squeeze the bottle. The diver will sink to the bottom. Let go, and it will float back up. With care, you can make it float at any depth you like!

What's happening?

When you squeeze the bottle, water is pushed into the straw, and the air in the straw is squeezed, or compressed. This makes the diver heavier. Its density increases, so it sinks. When you let go, the pressure of the air trapped in the straw pushes the water back out. This makes the diver less dense than water, so it floats up.

SINK OR SWIM

Sharks are never still in the water—they swim all the time. This is because they are denser than water, so if they stopped swimming, they would sink.

Acceleration

Forces can make things speed up, or accelerate. If the forces on an object are balanced, it will not change speed. But if the force pushing an object forward is greater than the force pushing it back, it will go faster and faster until the forces are balanced again. Unbalanced forces can make things change speed or direction.

Paddleboat

This paddleboat shows how unbalanced forces can push something forward.

YOU WILL NEED
20
- A TWO-LITER PLASTIC BOTTLE
- TWO STICKS, ABOUT 9 IN. (23CM) LONG
- A FLAT-SIDED PLASTIC CONTAINER
- SCISSORS
- WATERPROOF TAPE
- A RUBBER BAND, ABOUT 3.5 IN. (9CM) LONG

1 Cut four rectangles from the flat sides of the plastic container, 2 in. (5cm) by 3 in. (8cm) each.

Can you make your boat go backward?

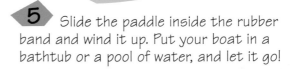

2 Fold the rectangles in half. Stand them on their long sides. Bring the folded edges together, making a cross shape. Tape them together to make a paddle.

5 Slide the paddle inside the rubber band and wind it up. Put your boat in a bathtub or a pool of water, and let it go!

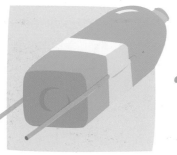

3 Tape the two sticks to opposite sides of the bottle, about three fourths of the way down, so they stick out about 3 in. (8cm).

4 Stretch the rubber band over the sticks. Use one that fits easily without being tightly stretched.

What's happening?

The boat is powered by the energy stored in the rubber band when you wind it up. As the paddle turns, it pushes against the water, making the forces on the bottle unbalanced. It accelerates until the resistance of the water pushing back is equal to the force of the paddle pushing forward, and the forces are balanced again. Then it moves at a steady speed until the rubber band runs out of stored energy.

Balloon boat

Stretch the balloon by blowing it up a few times. Tape the neck of the balloon to the straw—make sure the seal is airtight. Make a small hole in one end of the tray, big enough to fit the straw through. Put the straw through the hole, blow up the balloon, and seal the end of the straw with modeling clay. Put the boat in water and snip off the clay.

What's happening?
The balloon pushes air out through the straw, which pushes the boat forward. Jet engines and rockets work the same way, pushing an aircraft forward by shooting gases out from the back.

YOU WILL NEED
- A PLASTIC TRAY (THE KIND MICROWAVE DINNERS COME IN)
- A FLEXIBLE STRAW
- MODELING CLAY
- A BALLOON
- TAPE
- SCISSORS

10

FLASHBACK

Land speed record
The first land speed record was set in 1898 by Count Gaston de Chasseloup-Laubat of Paris, France. His car covered 0.6 miles (1km) in 57 seconds, averaging 39.14 mph (63.13km/h). Almost 100 years later, in 1997, the *Thrust SSC* supersonic car set a new record. Its twin turbojets accelerated *Thrust SSC* to 763.04 mph (1228.49km/h)—faster than the speed of sound. The streamlined shape helped it slice through the air with very little drag. Two sets of parachutes and special brakes were needed to bring it to a stop.

FAST FELINE
The cheetah holds the land speed record for animals. Its powerful legs and flexible spine allow it to accelerate to over 60 mph (100km/h).

Measuring speed

Measuring speed can be very useful. Car drivers, for example, need to know if they are staying below the safe speed limit. Railroad engineers need to know if they are going at the right speed to get to the next station at the right time. To find out how fast something is going, you need to know two things—the distance it has traveled and the time it has taken to do it.

Speed trial

Here is an easy way to measure how fast you ride your bike. Ask an adult to find a safe, traffic-free cycle path for this experiment.

YOU WILL NEED
- A BICYCLE
- A STOPWATCH OR A WATCH WITH A SECOND HAND
- A MEASURING TAPE
- A CALCULATOR
- A FRIEND

10

How fast can you cycle?

1 Measure the distance between two things along the side of the path (trees, for example). Try to choose things about 100 ft. (30m) apart.

2 Start cycling some distance back from the first post so you are going at a steady speed when you pass it. Ask your friend to time how long it takes you to travel from the first post to the second post.

$$\text{average speed} = \frac{\text{distance traveled}}{\text{time taken}}$$

What's happening?

Average speed tells you how far you went each second. For example, if you cycled 100 ft. in 5 seconds, your average speed was 100/5, which is 20 ft. per second, or 20 ft./s. Speed is often measured in miles per hour (mph), but the idea is the same.

3 Use this equation to figure out how fast you were going. If you measure the distance in feet and time in seconds, the answer will be in feet per second.

Balloon rocket race

Cut some straws into 4-in. (10-cm) lengths and thread them onto the end of the string. Tie the string between two chairs 30 ft. (9m) apart, pulling it tight. Blow up a balloon. Pinch the neck tightly, then ask a friend to tape it to the first piece of straw. Get your stopwatch ready and let go! Time how long the balloon takes to fly to the other end of the string. Compare different balloon shapes to see which goes fastest.

YOU WILL NEED
20
◆ A PACK OF BALLOONS OF DIFFERENT SHAPES
◆ DRINKING STRAWS
◆ TAPE
◆ STRING
◆ A MEASURING TAPE
◆ A STOPWATCH
◆ A FRIEND

Can you figure out the average speed of your balloon rockets?

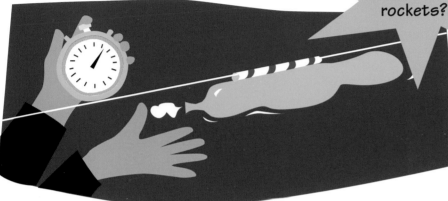

What's happening?

The balloon squeezes the air inside, forcing it out of the open end. This pushes the balloon forward. Long, thin balloons fly faster than round ones because they are a more streamlined shape and have to push less air out of the way as they go.

FLASHBACK

The tortoise and the hare

In this famous ancient Greek fable, a speedy hare challenges a slow tortoise to a race. The hare zooms off into the distance, but then stops for a nap. Meanwhile, the tortoise plods along steadily. The hare wakes up just as the tortoise is about to cross the finish line, and the hare loses the race. Although the hare's maximum speed was far faster than the tortoise's, his average speed over the whole race was slower.

PHOTO FINISH
When 1/100th second can make the difference between a gold and a silver medal, an invisible beam linked to special cameras records each runner's time more accurately than a person with a stopwatch ever could.

Friction

Whenever things rub together, friction is produced. Friction is an invisible force that tries to stop movement. It also occurs when something moves through a fluid, like water or air. Then it is often called drag. Sometimes friction is a useful force that provides grip or slows something down, but at other times it is a nuisance. Think about a bicycle—you lubricate moving parts like the chain to reduce friction, but it would be a big mistake to put oil on the wheel rims where the brake pads rub!

Slide or grip?

This quick experiment shows how the amount of friction between two surfaces depends on how rough or smooth they are.

YOU WILL NEED
- A LARGE WOODEN BOARD
- A SMOOTH PLASTIC TRAY
- AN ASSORTMENT OF FLAT-BOTTOMED, NONBREAKABLE OBJECTS, LIKE A PLASTIC CUP, A COIN, AN ERASER, AND A MATCHBOX

10

Why do some things slide more easily than others?

1 Line up your objects along one end of the wooden board. Which one do you think will slide most easily?

2 Slowly lift the end of the board until the objects move. Which slides most easily? Which sticks the most?

3 Now try using the plastic tray. Does it make a difference?

What's happening?

Some things slide along the wooden board more easily than others because there is less friction between their bottom surface and the board. They will probably be the objects that feel smoother to the touch. Things slide much more easily along a smooth surface like the plastic tray for the same reason.

Slippery ice

Try sliding your objects along the table one by one. Now try the same with an ice cube. What do you notice?

Which object slides most easily?

YOU WILL NEED
◆ YOUR FLAT-BOTTOMED OBJECTS FROM "SLIDE OR GRIP"
◆ A SMOOTH KITCHEN TABLE
◆ AN ICE CUBE

10

What's happening?

A thin layer of water from the melting ice reduces the amount of friction between the ice cube and the table, so it travels much more easily. The water acts as a lubricant, like the grease and oil between the moving parts of a machine. Water wouldn't normally be any good as a lubricant in a machine, though, because it would soon evaporate away and might make the machine parts rust.

Rubbing hands

Try rubbing the palms of your hands together, gently and slowly at first, then harder and more quickly. What do you notice? Make your hands wet and soapy, then try it again.

YOU WILL NEED
◆ SOAP
◆ WATER

5

What's happening?

The harder you press your hands together and the faster you rub, the hotter they feel. This is because rubbing your hands produces friction, and friction causes heat. When you do the same thing with wet, soapy hands, the water reduces the friction, so your hands feel less hot.

ICE SKATER
The narrow blade on an ice skate causes very high pressure underneath. This melts the ice, creating a thin layer of water that lubricates the blade. There is very little friction left to slow the skater down.

Air and water resistance

It takes a lot of effort to swim. This is because you have to push the water out of your way as you move forward. Then there's the friction of the water sliding against your skin, and the swirling water behind you trying to pull you back. Air has the same dragging effect, but you have to move faster before you really start to notice it. Drag isn't all bad, however. If your arms and legs slid through the water without any resistance, you wouldn't be able to push yourself forward in the first place!

Make a parachute

See how a simple parachute slows down a falling object. Ask an adult to help you get all the strings the same length.

YOU WILL NEED
- A PLASTIC BAG
- THREAD
- SCISSORS
- A PAPER CLIP
- A HOLE PUNCH
- SOMETHING TO USE AS A WEIGHT, LIKE MODELING CLAY OR A SMALL TOY

20

How does a parachute work?

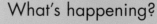

2 Tie one end of a 16-in. (40-cm) length of thread through the hole at each corner.

4 Drop the parachute from a safe height and see how long it takes to fall.

1 Cut out a 12-in. (30-cm) square from the plastic bag and punch a hole close to each corner.

3 Tie the other ends to the paper clip and add some modeling clay, or bend the paper clip to make a harness for your parachutist.

What's happening?

Parachutes work by creating a lot of air resistance. The big, curved canopy traps air underneath it, which pushes up against the canopy as it falls. The faster the parachute falls, the stronger the upward force trying to slow it down again.

Air resistance

Stand in an open space and drop your light objects one by one. Notice how they fall. Now get your sheets of tissue paper and scrunch one of them into a ball. Drop the sheet and the ball at the same time. What happens?

Why do some things fall faster than others?

YOU WILL NEED
- SEVERAL SMALL, LIGHT OBJECTS WITH BIG SURFACES FOR THEIR WEIGHT, SUCH AS A FEATHER, A LEAF, OR A PIECE OF THREAD
- TWO SHEETS OF TISSUE PAPER

⏱ 5

What's happening?

How fast something falls does not depend on how heavy it is. The sheet and the ball weigh the same, but the sheet falls less quickly because it has to push more air out of the way as it falls, and this air resistance makes it float down slowly. The compact ball moves through the air more easily, so it falls quickly.

Water resistance

Put both balls into the bowl of water so that they float. Try spinning one ball, and then the other. Which spins more easily?

YOU WILL NEED
- A BOWL OF WATER
- A TENNIS BALL
- A SMOOTH RUBBER BALL

⏱ 5

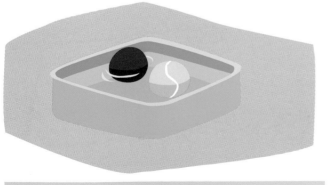

What's happening?

Water resists movement even more than air does. The rubber ball spins more easily because its smooth surface does not cause as much drag as the rough tennis ball.

GERONIMO!
When a parachute starts to fall, it accelerates until the upward force of air resistance balances the downward pull of gravity. It then falls at a steady speed, called its terminal velocity.

Floating in air

Because you cannot see air, it is easy to forget that it has weight. In fact, the atmosphere weighs a lot, as you can see from the air pressure experiment on page 14. Just like water, air causes an upward force on things, called upthrust. Believe it or not, if you put a weight on some scales and then take the air away, it will weigh more, in the same way that you weigh more when you let the water out of your bath. Something will float in air, just as in water, if the upthrust on it is equal to or more than its weight.

Make a hot-air balloon

This balloon is a little tricky to make, but it's a lot of fun! Ask an adult for help. Once you have made a working model, you can build a bigger one to scale.

YOU WILL NEED
- SHEETS OF TISSUE PAPER
- SCISSORS
- GLUE
- A HAIRDRYER
- FLEXIBLE STRAWS

20

1 Make a template in the shape shown, then use it to cut out eight pieces of tissue paper.

3 Ask an adult to fill the balloon with hot air using the hairdryer. If it flips upside down, strengthen the hole by gluing some flexible straws around the opening.

2 Using as little glue as you can, stick the edges together to make a balloon shape. It does not matter if you have to scrunch up the tissue a little to get it into the right shape, as long as there are no gaps left along the seams. A round patch of tissue paper will seal any gaps at the top.

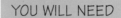
What makes your balloon fly?

What's happening?
Heating the air inside the balloon makes the air expand, pushing some out of the bottom. Now less air is taking up the same space, so it is less dense. The upthrust caused by the cooler, heavier air around the balloon makes it float up. As it cools down, the air in the balloon gets denser and heavier again, so the balloon comes down.

Hovering helium

Make a lot of identical weights by cutting up aluminum pie plates into ³/₄-in. (2-cm) squares. Using a straightened paper clip, carefully poke a hole through one corner of each weight. Tie a paper clip to the helium balloon with string and bend it to make a hanger for the weights. Attach the weights one at a time until the balloon can only just lift them. Every hour or so you will have to take some weights off to keep the balloon in the air.

YOU WILL NEED

10

◆ A FRESHLY FILLED HELIUM BALLOON (THE KIND THAT FLOATS UP TO THE CEILING)
◆ PAPER CLIPS
◆ STRING
◆ SOME EMPTY ALUMINUM PIE PLATES

What's happening?

Air is a mixture of gases—mostly nitrogen and oxygen—that are heavier than helium, which is a very light gas. A helium-filled balloon is lighter than air, so it floats up. The molecules of helium are so tiny, though, that after a while they start to leak out. The shrinking balloon gets heavier than air, and gravity pulls it back down.

FLASHBACK

The deck chair pilot

In 1982 former pilot Larry Walters decided to fly once more. He tied 45 helium-filled weather balloons to a deck chair and took off, hoping to float just above the ground. Instead, he shot into the sky to a height of almost 10,500 feet (3,200m). After 14 cold, terrifying hours he drifted past an airliner, whose pilot reported seeing a man in a deck chair at 9,840 feet (3,000m)! Mr. Walters was blown out to sea and was finally rescued by a helicopter, which towed him to safety.

UP, UP, AND AWAY
A hot-air balloon carries a powerful burner that heats the air inside the balloon. The cooler, denser air outside the balloon causes upthrust, which lifts the balloon skyward. Regular blasts of heat are needed to keep the balloon afloat.

Flight

There are other ways to create upward forces on things to make them fly besides using hot air or a light gas like helium. Birds and flying insects use flapping wings to give them lift, pushing the air down and behind them to move forward through the air. Airplanes use the same idea, but have fixed wings and propellers or jet engines to push them forward. The lift comes from the shape of the wings. Rockets work by blasting hot gases from the tail to push the rocket forward, even in the airless vacuum of space.

Make a rocket

This water rocket is a lot of fun, but you will need an adult to help make it and supervise the launch.

YOU WILL NEED
- A PLASTIC SOFT DRINK BOTTLE
- A CORK OR BUNG THAT FITS THE BOTTLE
- BALSA WOOD
- A DRILL WITH A SMALL BIT (ASK AN ADULT)
- A BICYCLE PUMP WITH CONNECTOR
- A NEEDLE ADAPTOR (THE KIND USED TO BLOW UP BASKETBALLS AND FOOTBALLS)
- STRONG GLUE

25

1 Cut out three or four fins from balsa wood in the shape shown and glue them to the bottle. The rocket should be able to stand on its fins. Let the glue dry.

3 Fill the bottle about one-fourth full with water and push the cork in hard.

2 Ask an adult to drill a small hole through the cork and push the needle adaptor in from the wide end. It needs to be a tight fit.

4 Take your rocket to the middle of an open space like a field, far away from buildings or overhead wires. Attach the connector and bicycle pump to the needle adaptor. Stand as far back as possible and pump air into the bottle. Pressure will build up until the cork pops out and the rocket blasts off!

Make a glider

Follow the diagrams to fold the paper. Add a paper clip to the nose, then throw your glider gently. Experiment by moving the paper clip to see which position makes the glider fly the farthest.

YOU WILL NEED
◆ A SHEET OF PAPER
◆ A PAPER CLIP
 10

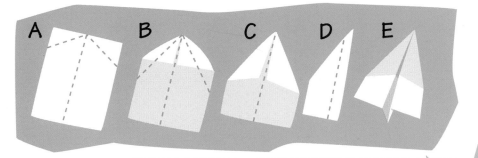

A B C D E

What's happening?
The glider flies a long way because of air resistance pushing up against the flat wings, opposing the pull of gravity.

Make a gyrocopter

Draw the shape shown. Cut along the heavy lines and fold the side strips out to make wings. Attach a paper clip to the bottom of your gyrocopter, then throw it up into the air.

YOU WILL NEED
◆ A PENCIL AND RULER
◆ PAPER OR THIN CARDBOARD
◆ SCISSORS
◆ A PAPER CLIP
10

What happens if you make one twice as big?

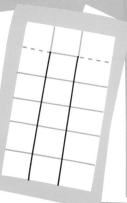

What's happening?
A gyrocopter is a helicopter without a motor. Air resistance causes the wings to spin as it falls. The spinning wings create lift, which works in the opposite direction to gravity and slows down its fall. Sycamore trees use the same trick to spread their seeds. The bigger the gyrocopter, the slower it falls.

What's happening?
Pumping air into the bottle increases the pressure inside until it overcomes the friction holding the cork in the neck of the bottle. The air and water blasting out of the bottom causes a reaction force that pushes the rocket up into the sky.

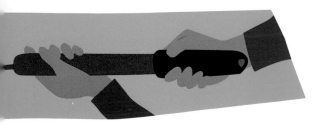

CRUISING CONDOR
Birds are masters of flight. Condors flap their wings to take off and gain height. Then they can glide for long distances. The shape of their wings gives them lift, and they can ride on rising columns of warmer air, called thermals, for hours.

Force magnifiers

How would you get the lid off a can of paint? You could use a screwdriver or something similar as a lever. Think about a doorknob. You push the handle a long way to make the latch move only a little to open the door. In both cases, a small force is used to move one end a long way, causing a big force to move something a short distance at the other end. Levers, doorknobs, and pulleys are called "force magnifiers."

Pulley power
Delight your friends with this demonstration of your superhuman strength!

YOU WILL NEED
- TWO BROOMS OR MOPS
- A FEW YARDS OF ROPE
- TALCUM POWDER
- A FEW FRIENDS

10

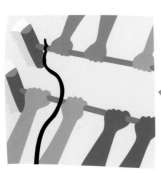

1 Tie the rope near the end of one broom.

2 Dust the two broom handles with talcum powder to reduce friction.

3 Get two or even four friends to hold the two brooms apart.

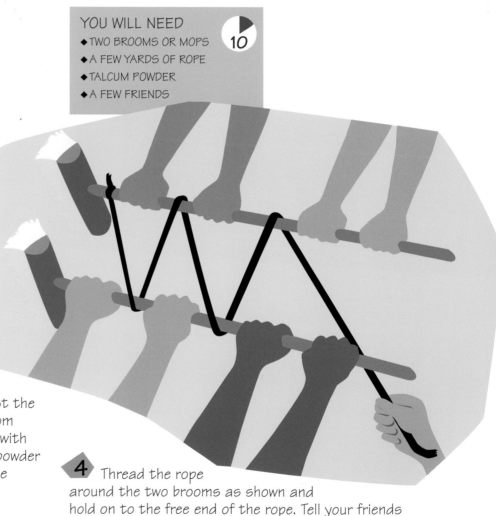

4 Thread the rope around the two brooms as shown and hold on to the free end of the rope. Tell your friends to try to keep the brooms apart with all their strength while you effortlessly pull them together!

What's happening?
Because of the way the rope is threaded between the brooms, pulling the free end a long way with a small force causes a huge force to tug the brooms a little way together. The broom handles are acting like pulleys. The more times the rope loops back and forth, the greater the force-magnifying effect.

Make a double pulley

Ask an adult to cut a coat hanger into two pieces and bend them to hold the spools and toy bucket as shown. Hang the wire without the bucket from a hook, attach the string as shown, and thread it around all the pulleys. Try lifting some weights with your double pulley.

YOU WILL NEED
- FOUR SPOOLS
- A WIRE COAT HANGER
- STRING
- A TOY BUCKET
- THINGS TO PUT IN THE BUCKET
- WIRE CUTTERS

20

Is it easy to lift the bucket?

What's happening?

The double pulley works just like the broom trick. Pulling the string a long way with a small force lifts the weight a little way with a big force, so the bucket is easy to lift.

Levers

Ask an adult to bang the lid onto the tin so that it's really tight. Try levering it off, first with the handle of a teaspoon, then with the dessert spoon handle. Be careful not to bend the spoons!

YOU WILL NEED
- A TIN WITH A TIGHT LID, LIKE A COCOA TIN
- A TEASPOON
- A DESSERT SPOON

5

What's happening?

The longer a lever is, the greater the turning force it can cause. The spoon handle is the lever, and the rim of the tin is the fulcrum. When you press on the spoon, your hand moves a long way with a small force. The end of the handle pushes the lid up a small way with a big force.

LOAD LIFTER
A wheelbarrow is a force magnifier. The wheel is the fulcrum, and the handles are the lever. By lifting the handles a long distance with a small force, you can lift a heavy load a little bit off the ground with a big force.

Gears

Gears are wheels with teeth around the outside. They can be connected directly together or joined by a chain. Depending on the sizes of the gear wheels, gears can be used as force magnifiers or movement magnifiers. They are used in all kinds of machines to change the speed or direction of movement. Bicycles and cars need gears to cope with going up and down hills and traveling at different speeds.

Bicycle gears

This experiment will show you the effect that gears have on a bicycle's movement.

YOU WILL NEED
◆ A BICYCLE WITH GEARS
◆ A TAPE MEASURE
◆ SOME CHALK
◆ A QUIET, LEVEL PATH AWAY FROM TRAFFIC

10

1 Put the bicycle into its lowest gear.

2 Make a chalk mark on the path where the back wheel touches the ground.

3 Gently turn the pedals one full turn, walking the bicycle forward in a straight line. Make a second mark next to the back wheel. Measure the distance between the marks.

How do bicycle gears work?

4 Put the bicycle into high gear and repeat the experiment. How far does it go this time?

What's happening?

The lowest gear works as a force magnifier. The pedals turn quickly compared to the wheel. It is very slow on flat ground, but good for climbing hills. High gear is a movement magnifier for pedaling downhill or going fast on level ground. The wheel turns quickly compared to the pedals, but with less power.

Making gears

Mark the center of each lid and ask an adult to punch a hole through it. Glue a spool onto each lid, in line with the hole. Stretch a thick rubber band around the rim of each lid to give it grip. Push two nails through the cardboard, spaced so that when you slot two lids over them, the lid rims just touch. Turn the larger lid and watch how the smaller lid moves. Try some different combinations of lid sizes; you could even arrange three lids in a row. You will have to move the nails each time you change the lids.

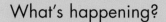

YOU WILL NEED
- WIDE RUBBER BANDS
- THICK CARDBOARD
- A HAMMER AND TWO 1½-IN. (4-CM) NAILS
- SPOOLS
- JAR LIDS OF VARIOUS SIZES

20

What's happening?

The lids act like the high gear on a bicycle, only without the chain to link the two gear wheels. Turning the large wheel slowly makes the small wheel spin quickly, without much force, in the opposite direction. You can change it into a model of low gear by using the small wheel to turn the larger wheel. Now the big wheel turns slowly with a lot of force.

FLASHBACK

Harrison's chronometer

Gears are not only useful on big machines like bicycles. The mechanism of a clock uses precision gears to steadily turn the hands at exactly the right speed. The first reliable portable clock, the H4 chronometer, was built nearly 250 years ago by English watchmaker John Harrison. With its intricate mechanism of gears and springs, H4 could keep good time, even on a tossing ship at sea. This was a huge breakthrough. By keeping accurate track of the time, sailors could figure out their precise position. It took Harrison 40 years to develop the H4, but it was worth it—he was awarded a large sum of money for his achievement.

BUILT FOR SPEED
Chris Boardman won an Olympic gold medal in 1992 riding this specially designed bike. The chainring gearwheel is much bigger than the one on the back wheel, so it acts like a very high gear. The bike and rider are streamlined, so they glide easily through the air.

Circular motion

Anything that spins around has circular motion. Moving things will always go in a straight line unless there is a force tugging them off course. When something moves in a circle, it is constantly changing direction. For this to happen, there has to be a force pulling it toward the middle of the circle. Scientists call this centripetal force. You can easily feel this force on a playground merry-go-round, tugging on your arms as your body tries to fly off in a straight line!

Spinning force

This experiment shows how centripetal force increases the faster something spins around. Find a space away from other people to do this!

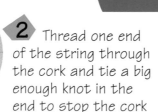

What happens to the weight when the cork whirls around?

YOU WILL NEED
- A CORK OR RUBBER BUNG **10**
- ABOUT 3 FT. (1M) OF STRING
- A SPOOL
- A SMALL WEIGHT, LIKE A WOODEN BLOCK
- A DRILL (ASK AN ADULT)

1 Ask an adult to drill a small hole lengthwise through the cork.

2 Thread one end of the string through the cork and tie a big enough knot in the end to stop the cork from sliding off.

3 Thread the other end of the string through the spool and tie it to the weight.

4 Holding on to the spool, start whirling the cork around in a circle, slowly at first and then faster and faster.

What's happening?

The cork is trying to fly off in a straight line. As it spins faster, the centripetal force needed to keep it moving in a circle increases. The tension in the string caused by these opposing forces pulls the weight up. The faster you spin the cork, the higher the weight is lifted.

Make a top

Use the compass to draw a circle on the cardboard and cut it out. Carefully push the pointed end of a pencil through the center of the circle. Spin the pencil on a smooth, flat surface.

YOU WILL NEED
◆ CARDBOARD OR THIN, STIFF PLASTIC
◆ A COMPASS
◆ SCISSORS
◆ A PENCIL
10

What's happening?

Spinning objects like wheels and gyroscopes resist being tilted. This makes them very stable. The cardboard circle helps the pencil balance on its point, especially if the center of gravity is kept low by having the card low down on the pencil.

Antigravity water

Tie the string to the bucket's handle. Half fill the bucket with water. Hold the string and lift the bucket so that it hangs just above the ground. Start turning around, very slowly at first, then faster and faster. Watch what happens to the water as the bucket moves higher into the air.

YOU WILL NEED
◆ A SMALL BUCKET WITH A HANDLE
◆ STRONG STRING OR ROPE
◆ AN OPEN SPACE OUTSIDE
10

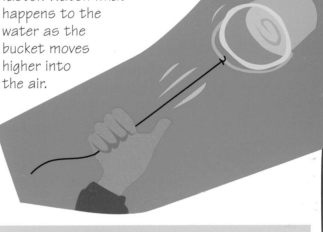

What's happening?

Centripetal force affects liquids, too. As the bucket spins, the water is trying to go in a straight line. The bottom of the bucket keeps pushing the water in toward the middle of the circle, and the water gets pressed against the bottom of the bucket, so it can't spill out. The water stays inside the bucket, even when the bucket is on its side!

AROUND AND AROUND

Spinning amusement park rides work by upsetting your sense of gravity. This one spins you around like the bucket of water, so that you can't tell up from down. Your body tries to fly off in a straight line, but the ride holds you in and pulls you around in a circle.

Starting and stopping

It takes a push or a pull to start something moving or to make it stop. Imagine pushing a heavy shopping cart. You have to push hard to start it moving, but once you've got it going, it will keep going by itself, even if you let go. You have to pull back on the handle to make it stop. This tendency of things to stay still if they're still, or to keep moving if they're already moving, is called inertia. The more mass something has, the greater its inertia.

Don't lose your marbles

This simple experiment shows how inertia affects the motion of some marbles in a shoebox lid. You will need to use a smooth, level floor.

YOU WILL NEED
10
- A FEW MARBLES OF VARIOUS SIZES
- A SHOEBOX LID
- TAPE
- A SKATEBOARD OR A TOY WITH WHEELS

1 Use tape to attach the lid firmly to the top of the skateboard and put it on the floor.

2 Put the marbles in the lid so they are spaced apart from one another.

What happens if the skateboard stops suddenly?

4 Stop the skateboard by pulling back on it. What happens to the marbles?

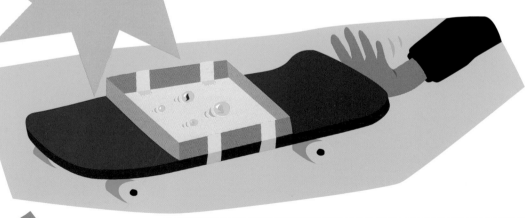

3 Give the skateboard a gentle push. Watch carefully what happens to the marbles.

What's happening?
Because they have inertia, the marbles try to stay still as you push the skateboard forward. They only start moving when the back wall of the lid gives them a push. When the skateboard stops, they try to keep moving forward and roll to the front of the lid. The heavier the marble is, the more inertia it has, and the more it resists any change in its motion.

Spinning egg puzzle

You can use this trick of inertia to find out if an egg is raw or cooked. Spin the cooked egg on its side, then stop it by gently grabbing it. Let go right away. It will stop, as you would expect. Try the same with the raw egg. What happens?

YOU WILL NEED

◆ A HARD-BOILED EGG   10
◆ A RAW EGG
◆ A SMOOTH PLATE

What's happening?

The liquid inside the raw egg has inertia, so it keeps on swirling around inside when you grab the shell. When you let go, it makes the whole egg start spinning again.

Demolish the tower

Build a tower of checkers near the edge of a smooth table. Put a ruler on the table next to the tower, with one end sticking out past the end of the table. Holding this end, slice the ruler quickly through the bottom of the tower by sliding it along the table with a flicking motion. With practice, you should be able to knock out the bottom checkers one by one without toppling the tower.

YOU WILL NEED
◆ CHECKERS   10
◆ A RULER
◆ A SMOOTH TABLE

What's happening?

The quick push needed to knock the bottom checker out is too small a force to overcome the inertia of the whole tower, which stays put. The magician's trick of whipping the tablecloth out from under some plates and glasses relies on inertia in the same way.

BUCKLE UP!
These inertia-reel seat belts unwind easily when you pull gently to put them on. If the car stops suddenly, the children's inertia will keep them moving forward. This tugs quickly on the seat belts, which instantly lock and hold the children safely in their seats.

Glossary

Acceleration   A change in an object's speed or direction. Scientists measure acceleration in meters per second squared.

Air pressure   The pressure caused by the weight of the atmosphere, also called atmospheric pressure. Although it is invisible, air has mass, so it is pulled down by the earth's gravity. The pressure of the air at the earth's surface is about 67.5 newtons per square inch, or ten newtons per square centimeter. Meteorologists track areas of higher or lower air pressure, because these have a strong effect on the weather.

Air resistance   The tendency of air to push back on objects traveling through it. This resistance happens because moving objects rub against the molecules of the gases that make up the air.

Balanced forces   Forces that do not cause any change in the motion of an object when they interact are said to be balanced. When you sit on a chair, for example, the force of gravity pulling you down is balanced by the force of the chair pushing you up.

Center of gravity (or center of mass)   The point in an object where the force of gravity appears to act. If it is suspended from any point on the vertical line passing through its center of gravity, the object will stay balanced.

Centripetal force   The force that causes something to move in a circular path. When you spin a weight around on a string, you have to pull on the string to keep the weight from flying off in a straight line. The force of the string tugging on the weight is the centripetal force.

Density   How much mass something has in relation to its volume. Density is worked out by dividing a substance's mass by its volume. Scientists measure density in grams per centimeter cubed.

Drag   An aerodynamic force that resists the forward motion of an object. The shape of the object affects the amount of drag.

Energy   The ability to do work. Work is done whenever a force moves through a distance— you can think of energy as a "promise" to do work. There are several kinds of energy, like light, heat, electrical, and potential energy.

Force   A push or pull that can change something's speed, shape, or direction. Forces are measured in newtons (N).

Force magnifier   A machine where a small force moving a long distance causes a big force to move a small distance—for example, a doorknob.

Friction   The rubbing force that resists movement when things slide against each other.

Fulcrum   The support around which a lever turns. The support in the middle of a seesaw is a fulcrum.

Gears   Toothed wheels used in machines to make one wheel turn another.

Gravitational pull   The pull of one object on another due to the force of gravity. For example, the gravitational pull of the earth keeps satellites in orbit.

Gravity   A force of attraction that pulls everything toward everything else. The strength of attraction depends on the mass of the objects and how far apart they are.

Inertia   The tendency of any object to stay still or move steadily in a straight line, unless a force makes it do otherwise. The more mass something has, the greater its inertia.

Kilogram   The standard unit of mass used in science. A volume of one liter of water has a mass of one kilogram.

Lever   A rigid bar that can turn on a fulcrum or hinge to transmit a force from one place to another. Wheelbarrows, scissors, and the muscles, bones, and joints of your body are all examples of lever systems.

Lift   An aerodynamic force caused by the motion of a wing through the air. Lift allows an airplane to climb into the air and holds it up during flight.

Lubricant   A substance that reduces the friction between two surfaces.

Machine   A device that does work. Machines are designed to make life easier for us.

Mass   The amount of material an object contains.

Motion   Motion occurs when something changes its position.

Movement magnifier   A machine that allows a large force moving a short distance to cause a small force to move a long distance—for example, the pedal that opens the lid of step-on trash can.

Newton   The unit for measuring forces. The pull of the earth's gravity on a mass of 3½ ounces (100g) is almost exactly 1N.

Potential energy   Energy that is stored. When you lift something up or stretch a spring, you give it potential energy.

Pressure   How concentrated or spread out a force is over a surface. Pressure is calculated by dividing the size of the force by the area it is acting on. Scientists measure it in pascals (Pa), or newtons per square meter.

Pulley   A wheel with a grooved rim that is used with a rope or a chain to make it easier to lift a heavy load. This is an example of a force magnifier.

Speed   How fast something is going. Speed is calculated by dividing distance by time. Average speed is the total distance traveled on a journey divided by the total time taken.

Streamlined   Shaped to reduce drag. A fish has a streamlined shape.

Turning force   The strength of a turning effect. The longer a lever, the greater the turning force it can produce.

Unbalanced forces   Forces that cause a change in the motion or shape of an object because the force acting in one direction is greater than the force acting in the opposite direction.

Upthrust   The upward force that acts on an object when it is immersed in a fluid. The size of the force is the same as the weight of the fluid that makes way for the object.

Weight   The force of gravity pulling on a mass on or near the surface of a planet.

Index

Photography Credits

Telegraph Colour Library 7, 13, 37

Powerstock/Zefa 9

NASA 11

Rex Features Ltd. 15, 25

Gettyone Stone 17, 19, 27

Empics 21, 23, 33

Bruce Coleman Collection 29

Arena Images 35

Image Bank 31